Hope

A Word Study Devotional

Written by
Nate Herron

Designed by
Tammy Herron

Word Study
DEVOTIONALS

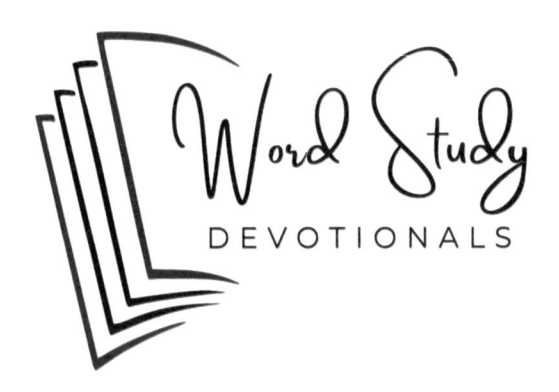

wordstudydevotionals.com

Scripture quotations taken from the (NASB®) New American Standard Bible®, Copyright © 2020 by The Lockman Foundation. Used by permission. All rights reserved. www.lockman.org.
Designed in the United States of America and printed in China.

Now may the God of hope fill you with all joy and peace in believing, so that you will abound in hope by the power of the Holy Spirit.
Romans 15:13

Table of Contents

Hope in the Old Testament

Israel's Hope 11
Hope in Despair 14
A Foolish Life is Hopeless 16
Hope in God's Word 18
Hope in Dark Times 20
Hope and Flourishing 22
True Hope Comes from Wisdom 24
Misplaced Hope 26
Counseling with Hope 30
Hope for Deliverance 33
Hope for the Downcast 36
God is Our True Hope 38
Fading Hope 40
Hope for the Living 44

Hope in the New Testament

Hope Beyond the Law 49
The Hope of the Gentiles 52
Daily Living in Hope 54
Hope in God's Promises 56
Hope and Love 60
Hope for Maturity 62
The Encouragement of Hope 64
Misplaced Hope 66
Hope to Be with You 68
Hope in a Glorious Future 72
Hope for Deliverance 76
Losing Hope 78
Hope of the Resurrection 80
Hope in Service 84

What is a Word Study Devotional?

A "word study" is a particular method of studying the Bible where you track a word or a short phrase throughout the Bible. By doing so, you discover how that word or phrase is described and developed by the biblical authors. It is often beautiful to see how cohesive, and nuanced, and layered the Bible can be as you trace a word through its pages.

Take the word "inheritance", for example. This word appears 230 times in the NASB version of the Bible. The vast majority of those appearances are in the Old Testament (212 times). Most of those speak of the nation and the land of Israel. But in the New Testament, the emphasis changes. By looking at just three instances of the word "inheritance" in the book of Ephesians, we see some of the richness that can come through word study. In Ephesians 1:11 we are told,

"In Him we also have obtained an **inheritance**, having been predestined according to the purpose of Him who works all things in accordance with the plan of His will."

This speaks of the believer's incredible heavenly inheritance which makes all the trials of this life pale in comparison. Then, just a few verses later, in Ephesians 1:13-14 we are shown a new aspect of our inheritance:

"In Him, you also, after listening to the message of truth, the gospel of your salvation—having also believed, you were sealed in Him with the Holy Spirit of the promise, who is a first installment of our **inheritance**, in regard to the redemption of God's own possession, to the praise of His glory."

Here we discover that the Holy Spirit seals us as a guarantee of the promise of our inheritance. Not only that, but the Holy Spirit Himself is a first installment, or a down payment, of our inheritance. We not only have a future heavenly inheritance, but we can experience some of the riches of our inheritance right now through the Holy Spirit sealing us and working in our lives!

Then, four verses later, Paul turns this concept of an inheritance around in a surprising way:

"I pray that the eyes of your heart may be enlightened, so that you will know what is the hope of His calling, what are the riches of the glory of His **inheritance** in the saints, and what is the boundless greatness of His power toward us who believe."

Here, in a dramatic reversal, the saints are called Jesus' inheritance! What a beautiful picture to comprehend that Jesus is our glorious inheritance, and we are His inheritance as well! We delight in Him and He delights in us!

There is so much to appreciate and to ponder from just these three instances of the word "inheritance". Insights and meditations like this abound from word studies in the Bible!

The Concept of this Book

Hope: A Word Study Devotional is an exhaustive word study of the word **hope**. Every single instance of the word hope in the Bible is presented in the following pages. This also includes derivative words such as hopeful, hopeless, hoping, hoped, etc. There are 144 instances of hope (or a derivative) in the New American Standard version of the Bible (NASB). There are 61 instances in the Old Testament and 83 instances in the New Testament.

In this book, each instance of the word hope is presented with sufficient context to help understand its meaning and usage. The verses have been organized and presented by theme to help connect instances of hope that relate to one another.

Commentary is purposefully not provided in each section. We want the Bible to speak for itself and for the readers to draw their own conclusions about hope from this word study.

How to Read this Book

The book is presented in a devotional format. Each section can be read in a brief amount of time, leaving room for meditation, prayer, and reflection. Each section presents a small number of verses meant to be read slowly and considered deeply.

As you consider the word hope in each section, its meaning, depth, and impact will grow and develop day by day. This is especially true when considering how the concept of hope expands from the Old Testament to the New Testament, as well as how it is explored within the various thematic sections.

At the end of each section, you will find one or two reflection questions. Feel free to use this space to journal your thoughts and ideas about hope, as well as to keep any extra notes you may have.

By the end of this book, you should have a great sense of the biblical meaning of hope!

Hope Defined

verb

- to desire with expectation of obtainment or fulfillment
- to expect with confidence : trust
- to cherish a desire with anticipation
- to want something to happen or be true

noun

- desire accompanied by expectation of or belief in fulfillment
- someone or something on which hopes are centered
- something desired or hoped for

Hope in the Old Testament

Ruth 1:12

II Kings 3:10, 4:28, 6:15

I Chronicles 29:15

Ezra 10:2

Esther 9:1

Job 4:6, 5:16, 6:8, 6:19, 7:6, 8:13, 11:18, 11:20, 13:15, 14:7, 14:19, 17:13, 17:15, 19:10, 27:8

Psalms 9:18, 33:17, 39:7, 62:5, 71:5, 119:49, 119:116, 119:166, 130:6, 146:5

Proverbs 10:28, 11:7, 13:12, 19:18, 23:18, 24:14, 26:12, 29:20

Ecclesiastes 9:4

Isaiah 20:5, 20:6, 38:18, 49:23, 57:10, 59:9, 59:11

Jeremiah 2:25, 13:16, 14:8, 17:13, 18:12, 29:11, 31:17, 50:7

Lamentations 3:18, 3:29

Ezekiel 19:5, 37:11

Hosea 2:15

Zechariah 9:5, 9:12

Hope in the New Testament

Matthew 12:21

Luke 23:8, 24:21

John 5:45

Acts 2:26, 16:19, 23:6, 24:15, 24:26, 26:6, 26:7, 27:20, 28:20

Romans 4:18, 5:2, 5:4, 5:5, 8:20, 8:24, 8:25, 12:12, 15:4, 15:12, 15:13, 15:24

I Corinthians 9:10, 13:7, 13:13, 15:19, 16:7

II Corinthians 1:7, 1:10, 1:13, 3:12, 5:11, 10:15

Galatians 5:5

Ephesians 1:12, 1:18, 2:12, 4:4

Philippians 1:20, 2:19, 2:23

Colossians 1:5, 1:23, 1:27

I Thessalonians 1:3, 2:19, 4:13, 5:8

II Thessalonians 2:16

I Timothy 1:1, 3:14, 4:10, 5:5, 6:17

Titus 1:2, 2:13, 3:7

Philemon 1:22

Hebrews 3:6, 6:11, 6:18, 6:19, 7:19, 10:23, 11:1

I Peter 1:3, 1:13, 1:21, 3:5, 3:15

I John 3:3, II John 1:12, III John 1:14

Hope

in the Old Testament

Israel's Hope

Jeremiah 29:10-14
10 "For this is what the Lord says: 'When seventy years have been completed for Babylon, I will visit you and fulfill My good word to you, to bring you back to this place. 11 For I know the plans that I have for you,' declares the Lord, 'plans for prosperity and not for disaster, to give you a future and a hope. 12 Then you will call upon Me and come and pray to Me, and I will listen to you. 13 And you will seek Me and find Me when you search for Me with all your heart. 14 I will let Myself be found by you,' declares the Lord, 'and I will restore your fortunes and gather you from all the nations and all the places where I have driven you,' declares the Lord, 'and I will bring you back to the place from where I sent you into exile.'

Jeremiah 31:15-19
15 This is what the Lord says:
"A voice is heard in Ramah,
Lamenting and bitter weeping.
Rachel is weeping for her children;
She refuses to be comforted for her children,
Because they are no more."
16 This is what the Lord says:
"Restrain your voice from weeping
And your eyes from tears;
For your work will be rewarded," declares the Lord,
"And they will return from the land of the enemy.
17 There is hope for your future," declares the Lord,
"And your children will return to their own territory.
18 I have certainly heard Ephraim grieving,
'You have disciplined me, and I was corrected,
Like an untrained calf;
Bring me back that I may be restored,
For You are the Lord my God.
19 For after I turned back, I repented;
And after I was instructed, I slapped my thigh;
I was ashamed and also humiliated
Because I bore the shame of my youth.'

Israel's Hope

Hosea 2:14-17
14 "Therefore, behold, I am going to persuade her, bring her into the wilderness, and speak kindly to her. 15 Then I will give her her vineyards from there, and the Valley of Achor as a door of hope. And she will respond there as in the days of her youth, as in the day when she went up from the land of Egypt. 16 And it will come about on that day," declares the Lord, "That you will call Me my husband And no longer call Me my Baal. 17 For I will remove the names of the Baals from her mouth, so that they will no longer be mentioned by their names.

Zechariah 9:10-13
10 And I will eliminate the chariot from Ephraim
And the horse from Jerusalem;
And the bow of war will be eliminated.
And He will speak peace to the nations;
And His dominion will be from sea to sea,
And from the Euphrates River to the ends of the earth.
11 As for you also, because of the blood of My covenant with you,
I have set your prisoners free from the waterless pit.
12 Return to the stronghold, you prisoners who have the hope;
This very day I am declaring that I will restore double to you.
13 For I will bend Judah as My bow,
I will fill the bow with Ephraim.
And I will stir up your sons, Zion, against your sons, Greece;
And I will make you like a warrior's sword.

Ezekiel 37:11-13
11 Then He said to me, "Son of man, these bones are the entire house of Israel; behold, they say, 'Our bones are dried up and our hope has perished. We are completely cut off.' 12 Therefore prophesy and say to them, 'This is what the Lord God says: "Behold, I am going to open your graves and cause you to come up out of your graves, My people; and I will bring you into the land of Israel. 13 Then you will know that I am the Lord, when I have opened your graves and caused you to come up out of your graves, My people.

Reflection

What was Israel's hope, according to the prophets?

How do you think this hope affected the daily lives of the people of Israel?

Hope in Despair

Job 13:15
Though He slay me, I will hope in Him. Nevertheless I will argue my ways before Him.

Lamentations 3:16-33
16 He has also made my teeth grind with gravel; He has made me cower in the dust.
17 My soul has been excluded from peace; I have forgotten happiness.
18 So I say, "My strength has failed, and so has my hope from the Lord."
19 Remember my misery and my homelessness, the wormwood and bitterness.
20 My soul certainly remembers, and is bent over within me.
21 I recall this to my mind, therefore I wait.
22 The Lord's acts of mercy indeed do not end, for His compassions do not fail.
23 They are new every morning; great is Your faithfulness.
24 "The Lord is my portion," says my soul, "Therefore I wait for Him."
25 The Lord is good to those who await Him, to the person who seeks Him.
26 It is good that he waits silently for the salvation of the Lord.
27 It is good for a man to bear the yoke in his youth.
28 Let him sit alone and keep quiet, since He has laid it on him.
29 Let him put his mouth in the dust; perhaps there is hope.
30 Let him give his cheek to the one who is going to strike him; let him be filled with shame.
31 For the Lord will not reject forever,
32 For if He causes grief, then He will have compassion in proportion to His abundant mercy.
33 For He does not afflict willingly or grieve the sons of mankind.

Reflection

How did the writers of Lamentations and Job cling to sparks of hope in suffering? What enabled this?

Notes

A Foolish Life is *Hopeless*

Proverbs 26:12
Do you see a person wise in his own eyes? There is more hope for a fool than for him.

Proverbs 29:20
Do you see a person who is hasty with his words? There is more hope for a fool than for him.

Jeremiah 13:15-17
15 Listen and pay attention, do not be haughty; For the Lord has spoken. 16 Give glory to the Lord your God before He brings darkness and before your feet stumble on the mountains in the dark, and while you are hoping for light He makes it into gloom, and turns it into thick darkness. 17 But if you do not listen to it, my soul will weep in secret for such pride; and my eyes will shed and stream down tears, because the flock of the Lord has been taken captive.

Jeremiah 18:11-12
11 So now, speak to the men of Judah and against the inhabitants of Jerusalem, saying, 'This is what the Lord says: "Behold, I am forming a disaster against you and devising a plan against you. Now turn back, each of you from his evil way, and correct your ways and your deeds!"' 12 But they will say, 'It's hopeless! For we are going to follow our own plans, and each of us will persist in the stubbornness of his evil heart.'

Reflection

Why is hope difficult to attain when one lives apart from God's wisdom?

What changes in your mindset or in your actions can protect you from foolishness?

Hope in God's Word

Psalms 119:49-50
49 Remember the word to Your servant, in which You have made me hope.
50 This is my comfort in my misery, that Your word has revived me.

Psalms 119:113-117
113 I hate those who are double-minded,
but I love Your Law.
114 You are my hiding place and my shield;
I wait for Your word.
115 Leave me, you evildoers,
so that I may comply with the commandments of my God.
116 Sustain me according to Your word, that I may live;
and do not let me be ashamed of my hope.
117 Sustain me so that I may be safe,
that I may have regard for Your statutes continually.

Psalms 119:165-166
165 Those who love Your Law have great peace,
And nothing causes them to stumble.
166 I hope for Your salvation, Lord,
And do Your commandments.

Reflection

When has God's word been an anchor of hope for you in difficult seasons?

Are there Bible passages that have been especially meaningful to you in those times?

Hope in Dark Times

Ezra 10:1-4
1 Now while Ezra was praying and making confession, weeping and prostrating himself before the house of God, a very large assembly, men, women, and children, gathered to him from Israel; for the people wept greatly. 2 Shecaniah the son of Jehiel, one of the sons of Elam, said to Ezra, "We have been unfaithful to our God and have married foreign women from the peoples of the land; yet now there is hope for Israel in spite of this. 3 So now let's make a covenant with our God to send away all the wives and their children, following the counsel of my lord and of those who fear the commandment of our God; and let it be done according to the Law. 4 Arise! For this matter is your responsibility, but we will be with you; be courageous and act."

Jeremiah 14:7-8
7 Though our wrongdoings testify against us,
Lord, act for the sake of Your name!
Our apostasies have indeed been many,
We have sinned against You.
8 Hope of Israel,
Its Savior in time of distress,
Why are You like a stranger in the land,
Or like a traveler who has pitched his tent for the night?

Proverbs 19:18
Discipline your son while there is hope, and do not desire his death.

Reflection

What helps you hold onto hope when life feels despairing? How can God's word help sustain you?

When has God proven faithful to you in darkness? Thank Him today for sustaining you.

Hope and Flourishing

Proverbs 13:12
Hope deferred makes the heart sick, but desire fulfilled is a tree of life.

Ruth 1:10-14
10 However, they said to her, "No, but we will return with you to your people." 11 But Naomi said, "Return, my daughters. Why should you go with me? Do I still have sons in my womb, that they may be your husbands? 12 Return, my daughters! Go, for I am too old to have a husband. If I said I have hope, if I were even to have a husband tonight and also give birth to sons, 13 would you therefore wait until they were grown? Would you therefore refrain from marrying? No, my daughters; for it is much more bitter for me than for you, because the hand of the Lord has come out against me." 14 And they raised their voices and wept again; and Orpah kissed her mother-in-law, but Ruth clung to her.

Reflection

How does hope, or lack of hope, impact your motivation and outlook on life?

Notes

True Hope Comes from Wisdom

Proverbs 24:13-14
13 My son, eat honey, for it is good; yes, the honey from the comb is sweet to your taste; 14 Know that wisdom is the same for your soul; if you find it, then there will be a future, and your hope will not be cut off.

Jeremiah 17:13
Lord, the hope of Israel, all who abandon You will be put to shame. Those who turn away on earth will be written down, because they have forsaken the fountain of living water, that is the Lord.

Isaiah 59:8-13
8 They do not know the way of peace, and there is no justice in their tracks; they have made their paths crooked, whoever walks on them does not know peace. 9 Therefore justice is far from us, and righteousness does not reach us; we hope for light, but there is darkness, for brightness, but we walk in gloom. 10 We grope for the wall like people who are blind, we grope like those who have no eyes. We stumble at midday as in the twilight; among those who are healthy we are like the dead. 11 All of us growl like bears, and moan sadly like doves; we hope for justice, but there is none; for salvation, but it is far from us. 12 For our wrongful acts have multiplied before You, and our sins have testified against us; for our wrongful acts are with us, and we know our wrongdoings: 13 offending and denying the Lord, and turning away from our God, speaking oppression and revolt, conceiving and uttering lying words from the heart.

Reflection

How does wisdom lead to genuine hope instead of false hopes?

Notes

Misplaced Hope

Esther 9:1
Now in the twelfth month (that is, the month Adar), on the thirteenth day, when the king's command and edict were to be put into effect, on the day when the enemies of the Jews hoped to gain the mastery over them, it turned out to the contrary so that the Jews themselves gained mastery over those who hated them.

Isaiah 57:7-10
7 On a high and lofty mountain You have made your bed. You also went up there to offer sacrifice. 8 Behind the door and the doorpost you have set up your sign; Indeed, far removed from Me, you have uncovered yourself, and have gone up and made your bed wide. And you have made an agreement for yourself with them, you have loved their bed, you have looked at their manhood. 9 You have journeyed to the king with oil and increased your perfumes; You have sent your messengers a great distance and made them go down to Sheol. 10 You were tired out by the length of your road, yet you did not say, 'It is hopeless!' You found renewed strength, therefore you did not faint.

Jeremiah 2:23-25
23 "How can you say, 'I am not defiled, I have not gone after the Baals'? Look at your way in the valley! Know what you have done! You are a swift young camel running about senselessly on her ways, 24 A wild donkey accustomed to the wilderness, That sniffs the wind in her passion. Who can turn her away in her mating season? None who seek her will grow weary; In her month they will find her. 25 Keep your feet from being bare, And your throat from thirst; But you said, 'It is ==hopeless==! No! For I have loved strangers, And I will walk after them.'

Jeremiah 50:6-7
6 "My people have become lost sheep; Their shepherds have led them astray. They have made them turn aside on the mountains. They have gone from mountain to hill, they have forgotten their resting place. 7 All who found them have devoured them; and their adversaries have said, 'We are not guilty, since they have sinned against the Lord who is the habitation of righteousness, the Lord, the ==hope== of their fathers.'

Misplaced *Hope*

Zechariah 9:3-6
3 For Tyre built herself a fortress,
And piled up silver like dust,
And gold like the mud of the streets.
4 Behold, the Lord will dispossess her
And throw her wealth into the sea;
And she will be consumed with fire.
5 Ashkelon will see it and be afraid.
Gaza too will writhe in great pain;
Also Ekron, because her ==hope== has been ruined.
Moreover, the king will perish from Gaza,
And Ashkelon will not be inhabited.
6 And a people of mixed origins will live in Ashdod,
And I will eliminate the pride of the Philistines.

Ezekiel 19:1-5
1 "As for you, take up a song of mourning for the leaders of Israel 2 and say, 'What was your mother? A lioness among lions! She lay down among young lions, she raised her cubs. 3 When she brought up one of her cubs, he became a young lion, and he learned to tear his prey; he devoured people. 4 Then nations heard about him; he was caught in their trap, and they brought him with hooks to the land of Egypt. 5 When she saw, as she waited, that her ==hope== was lost, she took another of her cubs and made him a young lion.

Isaiah 20:3-6
3 Then the Lord said, "Even as My servant Isaiah has gone naked and barefoot for three years as a sign and symbol against Egypt and Cush, 4 so the king of Assyria will lead away the captives of Egypt and the exiles of Cush, young and old, naked and barefoot with buttocks uncovered, to the shame of Egypt. 5 Then they will be terrified and ashamed because of Cush their ==hope== and Egypt their pride. 6 So the inhabitants of this coastland will say on that day, 'Behold, such is our ==hope==, where we fled for help to be saved from the king of Assyria; and how are we ourselves to escape?'"

Reflection

What is the difference between genuine hope in God and misguided hopes? How can you distinguish between the two?

Ask God to reveal any empty hopes that you need to surrender to Him. What might it look like to hope in Him alone?

Counseling with *Hope*

Job 4:4-8 (Job's friend Eliphaz describing Job)
4 Your words have helped the stumbling to stand, and you have strengthened feeble knees.
5 But now it comes to you, and you are impatient; it touches you, and you are horrified.
6 Is your fear of God not your confidence, and the integrity of your ways your hope?
7 "Remember now, who ever perished being innocent? Or where were the upright destroyed?
8 According to what I have seen, those who plow wrongdoing and those who sow trouble harvest it.

Job 5:14-18
14 By day they meet with darkness, and grope at noon as in the night. 15 But He saves from the sword of their mouth, and the poor from the hand of the strong. 16 So the helpless has hope, and injustice has shut its mouth. 17 "Behold, happy is the person whom God disciplines, so do not reject the discipline of the Almighty. 18 For He inflicts pain, and gives relief; He wounds, but His hands also heal.

Job 8:11-15
11 "Can papyrus grow tall without a marsh? Can the rushes grow without water? 12 While it is still green and not cut down, yet it withers before any other plant. 13 So are the paths of all who forget God; and the hope of the godless will perish, 14 His confidence is fragile, and his trust is a spider's web. 15 He depends on his house, but it does not stand; he holds on to it, but it does not endure.

Job 11:16-20
16 For you would forget your trouble;Like waters that have passed by, you would remember it. 17 Your life would be brighter than noonday; Darkness would be like the morning. 18 Then you would trust, because there is hope; And you would look around and rest securely. 19 You would lie down and none would disturb you, And many would flatter you. 20 But the eyes of the wicked will fail, And there will be no escape for them; And their hope is to breathe their last."

Job 14:7-9

7 "For there is hope for a tree, When it is cut down, that it will sprout again, And its shoots will not fail.
8 Though its roots grow old in the ground, And its stump dies in the dry soil,
9 At the scent of water it will flourish And produce sprigs like a plant.

Reflection

When counseling others, how can you wisely redirect misplaced hopes to the better hope found in Christ?

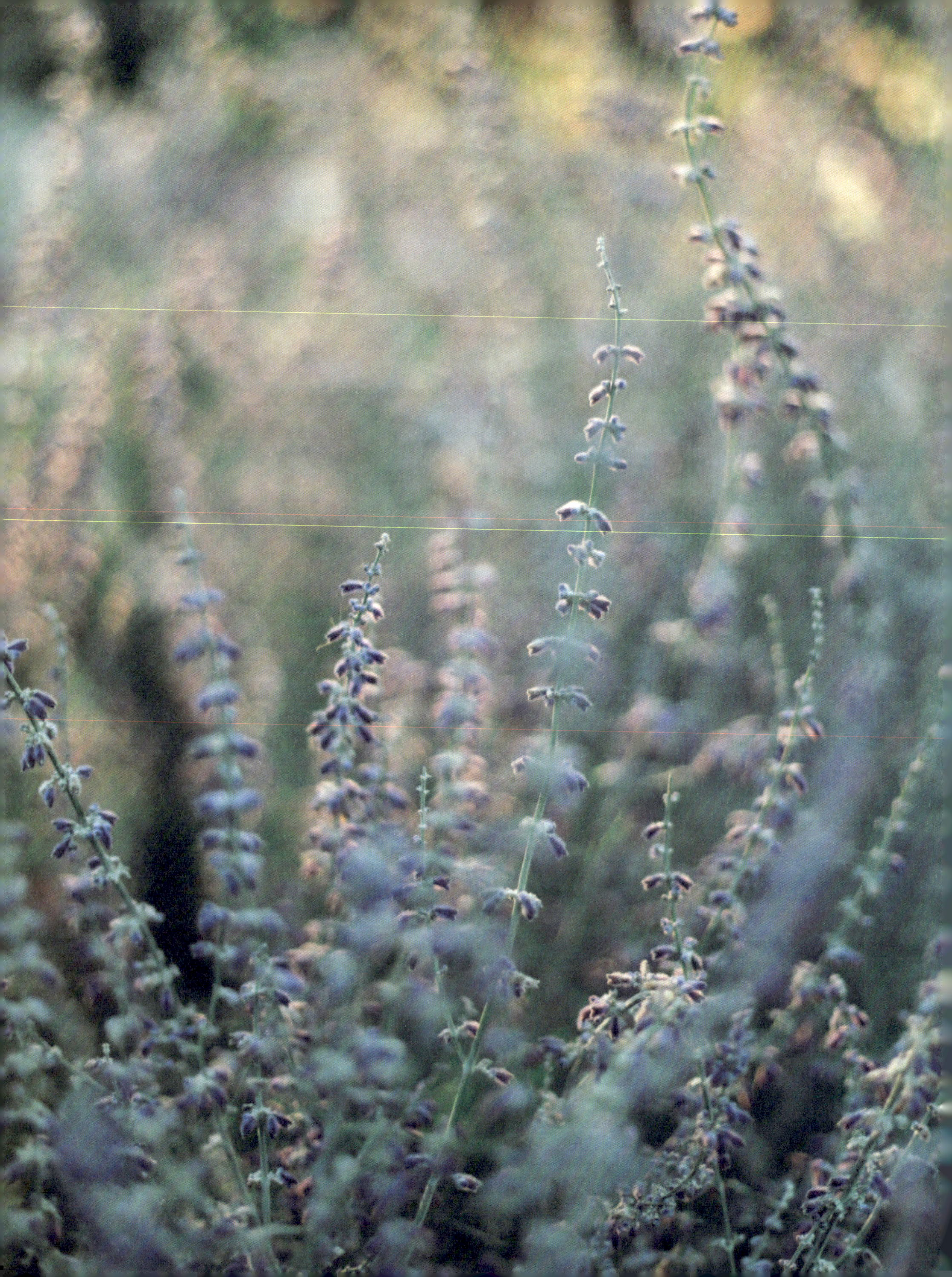

Hope for Deliverance

Psalms 146:3-8
3 Do not trust in noblemen,
In mortal man, in whom there is no salvation.
4 His spirit departs, he returns to the earth;
On that very day his plans perish.
5 Blessed is he whose help is the God of Jacob,
Whose hope is in the Lord his God,
6 Who made heaven and earth,
The sea and everything that is in them;
Who keeps faith forever;
7 Who executes justice for the oppressed;
Who gives food to the hungry.
The Lord frees the prisoners.
8 The Lord opens the eyes of those who are blind;
The Lord raises up those who are bowed down;
The Lord loves the righteous.

Psalms 71:4-6
4 Save me, my God, from the hand of the wicked,
From the grasp of the wrongdoer and the ruthless,
5 For You are my hope;
Lord God, You are my confidence from my youth.
6 I have leaned on you since my birth;
You are He who took me from my mother's womb;
My praise is continually of You.

Hope for Deliverance

Psalms 9:17-20
17 The wicked will return to Sheol,
All the nations who forget God.
18 For the needy will not always be forgotten,
Nor the hope of the afflicted perish forever.
19 Arise, Lord, do not let mankind prevail;
Let the nations be judged before You.
20 Put them in fear, Lord;
Let the nations know that they are merely human. Selah

Isaiah 49:22-24
22 This is what the Lord God says:
"Behold, I will lift up My hand to the nations
And set up My flag to the peoples;
And they will bring your sons in their arms,
And your daughters will be carried on their shoulders.
23 Kings will be your guardians,
And their princesses your nurses.
They will bow down to you with their faces to the ground
And lick the dust from your feet;
And you will know that I am the Lord;
Those who hopefully wait for Me will not be put to shame.
24 "Can the prey be taken from a mighty man,
Or the captives of a tyrant be rescued?"

Reflection

How has God proven Himself faithful to deliver His people in biblical history?

How does this give you hope for today?

Hope for the Downcast

Psalms 62:5-7
5 My soul, wait in silence for God alone,
For my hope is from Him.
6 He alone is my rock and my salvation,
My refuge; I will not be shaken.
7 My salvation and my glory rest on God;
The rock of my strength, my refuge is in God.

II Kings 3:9-12
9 So the king of Israel went with the king of Judah and the king of Edom, and they made a circuit of seven days' journey. But there was no water for the army or for the cattle that followed them. 10 Then the king of Israel said, "It is hopeless! For the Lord has called these three kings to hand them over to Moab!" 11 But Jehoshaphat said, "Is there no prophet of the Lord here, that we may inquire of the Lord by him?" And one of the king of Israel's servants answered and said, "Elisha the son of Shaphat is here, who used to pour water on the hands of Elijah." 12 And Jehoshaphat said, "The word of the Lord is with him." So the king of Israel and Jehoshaphat and the king of Edom went down to him.

II Kings 4:25-28
25 So she went on and came to the man of God at Mount Carmel. When the man of God saw her at a distance, he said to Gehazi his servant, "Behold, that person there is the Shunammite. 26 Please run now to meet her and say to her, 'Is it going well for you? Is it going well for your husband? Is it going well for the child?'" Then she answered, "It is going well." 27 But she came to the man of God at the hill and took hold of his feet. And Gehazi came up to push her away, but the man of God said, "Leave her alone, for her soul is troubled within her; and the Lord has concealed it from me and has not informed me." 28 Then she said, "Did I ask for a son from my lord? Did I not say, 'Do not give me false hope'?"

II Kings 6:15-17
15 Now when the attendant of the man of God had risen early and gone out, behold, an army with horses and chariots was circling the city. And his servant said to him, "This is hopeless, my master! What are we to do?" 16 And he said, "Do not be afraid, for those who are with us are greater than those who are with them." 17 Then Elisha prayed and said, "Lord, please, open his eyes so that he may see." And the Lord opened the servant's eyes, and he saw; and behold, the mountain was full of horses and chariots of fire all around Elisha.

Reflection

When you are discouraged, how can hope in God lift your soul?

God is Our True Hope

I Chronicles 29:10-16

10 So David blessed the Lord in the sight of all the assembly; and David said, "Blessed are You, Lord God of Israel our father, forever and ever. 11 Yours, Lord, is the greatness, the power, the glory, the victory, and the majesty, indeed everything that is in the heavens and on the earth; Yours is the dominion, Lord, and You exalt Yourself as head over all. 12 Both riches and honor come from You, and You rule over all, and in Your hand is power and might; and it lies in Your hand to make great and to strengthen everyone. 13 Now therefore, our God, we thank You, and praise Your glorious name. 14 But who am I and who are my people that we should be able to offer as generously as this? For all things come from You, and from Your hand we have given to You. 15 For we are strangers before You, and temporary residents, as all our fathers were; our days on the earth are like a shadow, and there is no hope. 16 Lord our God, all this abundance that we have provided to build You a house for Your holy name, it is from Your hand, and everything is Yours."

Psalms 33:16-19

16 The king is not saved by a mighty army;
A warrior is not rescued by great strength.
17 A horse is a false hope for victory;
Nor does it rescue anyone by its great strength.
18 Behold, the eye of the Lord is on those who fear Him,
On those who wait for His faithfulness,
19 To rescue their soul from death
And to keep them alive in famine.

Psalms 39:6-8

6 Certainly every person walks around as a fleeting shadow;
They certainly make an uproar for nothing;
He amasses riches and does not know who will gather them.
7 "And now, Lord, for what do I wait?
My hope is in You.
8 Save me from all my wrongdoings;
Do not make me an object of reproach for the foolish.

Reflection

Why is God alone the only sure source of hope?

How can you avoid placing hope elsewhere?

Fading Hope

Job 6:8-10
8 "Oh, that my request might come to pass,
And that God would grant my ==hope==!
9 Oh, that God would decide to crush me,
That He would let loose His hand and cut me off!
10 But it is still my comfort,
And I rejoice in unsparing pain,
That I have not denied the words of the Holy One.

Job 6:18-21
18 The paths of their course wind along,
They go up into wasteland and perish.
19 The caravans of Tema looked,
The travelers of Sheba ==hoped== for them.
20 They were put to shame, for they had trusted,
They came there and were humiliated.
21 Indeed, you have now become such,
You see terrors and are afraid.

Job 7:5-7
5 My flesh is clothed with maggots and a crust of dirt,
My skin hardens and oozes.
6 My days are swifter than a weaver's shuttle,
And they come to an end without ==hope==.
7 "Remember that my life is a mere breath;
My eye will not see goodness again.

Job 14:13-19
13 "Oh that You would hide me in Sheol,
That You would conceal me until Your wrath returns to You,
That You would set a limit for me and remember me!
14 If a man dies, will he live again?
All the days of my struggle I will wait
Until my relief comes.
15 You will call, and I will answer You;
You will long for the work of Your hands.
16 For now You number my steps,
You do not observe my sin.
17 My wrongdoing is sealed up in a bag,
And You cover over my guilt.
18 "But the falling mountain crumbles away,
And the rock moves from its place;
19 Water wears away stones,
Its torrents wash away the dust of the earth;
So You destroy a man's hope.

Job 17:13-16
13 If I hope for Sheol as my home,
I make my bed in the darkness;
14 If I call to the grave, 'You are my father';
To the maggot, 'my mother and my sister';
15 Where then is my hope?
And who looks at my hope?
16 Will it go down with me to Sheol?
Shall we together go down into the dust?"

Fading *Hope*

Job 19:8-11
8 He has blocked my way so that I cannot pass,
And He has put darkness on my paths.
9 He has stripped my honor from me
And removed the crown from my head.
10 He breaks me down on every side, and I am gone;
And He has uprooted my hope like a tree.
11 He has also kindled His anger against me
And considered me as His enemy.

Job 27:8
For what is the hope of the godless when he makes an end of life,
When God requires his life?

Reflection

When have you experienced fading hope? What restored your hope in God?

Notes

Hope for the Living

Isaiah 38:17-19
17 Behold, for my own welfare I had great bitterness;
But You have kept my soul from the pit of nothingness,
For You have hurled all my sins behind Your back.
18 For Sheol cannot thank You,
Death cannot praise You;
Those who go down to the pit cannot hope for Your faithfulness.
19 It is the living who give thanks to You, as I do today;
A father tells his sons about Your faithfulness.

Ecclesiastes 9:3-6
3 This is an evil in everything that is done under the sun, that there is one fate for everyone. Furthermore, the hearts of the sons of mankind are full of evil, and insanity is in their hearts throughout their lives. Afterward they go to the dead. 4 For whoever is joined to all the living, there is hope; for better a live dog, than a dead lion. 5 For the living know that they will die; but the dead do not know anything, nor do they have a reward any longer, for their memory is forgotten. 6 Indeed their love, their hate, and their zeal have already perished, and they will no longer have a share in all that is done under the sun.

Proverbs 10:28
The hope of the righteous is gladness,
But the expectation of the wicked perishes.

Proverbs 11:7
When a wicked person dies, his expectation will perish,
And the hope of strong people perishes.

Proverbs 23:17-19

17 Do not let your heart envy sinners,
But live in the fear of the Lord always.
18 Certainly there is a future,
And your hope will not be cut off.
19 Listen, my son, and be wise,
And direct your heart in the way.

Reflection

How should hope be a part of your daily experience?

Hope in Review

After considering what the Old Testament says about hope, what are some of the important lessons you are holding onto?

Are there ways to incorporate these truths into your life on a regular basis?

Study Notes

Hope

in the New Testament

Hope — Beyond the Law

Hebrews 7:15-19
15 And this is clearer still, if another priest arises according to the likeness of Melchizedek, 16 who has become a priest not on the basis of a law of physical requirement, but according to the power of an indestructible life. 17 For it is attested of Him, "You are a priest forever according to the order of Melchizedek." 18 For, on the one hand, there is the nullification of a former commandment because of its weakness and uselessness 19 (for the Law made nothing perfect); on the other hand, there is the introduction of a better hope, through which we come near to God.

John 5:43-47
43 I have come in My Father's name, and you do not receive Me; if another comes in his own name, you will receive him. 44 How can you believe, when you accept glory from one another and you do not seek the glory that is from the one and only God? 45 Do not think that I will accuse you before the Father; the one who accuses you is Moses, in whom you have put your hope. 46 For if you believed Moses, you would believe Me; for he wrote about Me. 47 But if you do not believe his writings, how will you believe My words?"

Galatians 5:1-6
1 It was for freedom that Christ set us free; therefore keep standing firm and do not be subject again to a yoke of slavery. 2 Look! I, Paul, tell you that if you have yourselves circumcised, Christ will be of no benefit to you. 3 And I testify again to every man who has himself circumcised, that he is obligated to keep the whole Law. 4 You have been severed from Christ, you who are seeking to be justified by the Law; you have fallen from grace. 5 For we, through the Spirit, by faith, are waiting for the hope of righteousness. 6 For in Christ Jesus neither circumcision nor uncircumcision means anything, but faith working through love.

Hope Beyond the Law

II Corinthians 3:9-14
9 For if the ministry of condemnation has glory, much more does the ministry of righteousness excel in glory. 10 For indeed what had glory in this case has no glory, because of the glory that surpasses it. 11 For if that which fades away was with glory, much more that which remains is in glory. 12 Therefore, having such a hope, we use great boldness in our speech, 13 and we are not like Moses, who used to put a veil over his face so that the sons of Israel would not stare at the end of what was fading away. 14 But their minds were hardened; for until this very day at the reading of the old covenant the same veil remains unlifted, because it is removed in Christ.

Notes

Reflection

Why does hope in Christ and grace surpass adherence to law?

How have you experienced this?

The Hope of the Gentiles

Matthew 12:18-21
18 "Behold, My Servant whom I have chosen;
My Beloved in whom My soul delights;
I will put My Spirit upon Him,
And He will proclaim justice to the Gentiles.
19 He will not quarrel, nor cry out;
Nor will anyone hear His voice in the streets.
20 A bent reed He will not break off,
And a dimly burning wick He will not extinguish,
Until He leads justice to victory.
21 And in His name the Gentiles will hope."

Romans 15:8-13
8 For I say that Christ has become a servant to the circumcision in behalf of the truth of God, to confirm the promises given to the fathers, 9 and for the Gentiles to glorify God for His mercy; as it is written: "Therefore I will give praise to You among the Gentiles, and I will sing praises to Your name." 10 Again he says, "Rejoice, you Gentiles, with His people." 11 And again, "Praise the Lord all you Gentiles, and let all the peoples praise Him." 12 Again Isaiah says, "There shall come the root of Jesse, and He who arises to rule over the Gentiles, in Him will the Gentiles hope." 13 Now may the God of hope fill you with all joy and peace in believing, so that you will abound in hope by the power of the Holy Spirit.

Ephesians 2:11-16
11 Therefore remember that previously you, the Gentiles in the flesh, who are called "Uncircumcision" by the so-called "Circumcision" which is performed in the flesh by human hands— 12 remember that you were at that time separate from Christ, excluded from the people of Israel, and strangers to the covenants of the promise, having no hope and without God in the world. 13 But now in Christ Jesus you who previously were far away have been brought near by the blood of Christ. 14 For He Himself is our peace, who made both groups into one and broke down the barrier of the dividing wall, 15 by abolishing in His flesh the hostility, which is the Law composed of commandments expressed in ordinances, so that in Himself He might make the two one new person, in this way establishing peace; 16 and that He might reconcile them both in one body to God through the cross, by it having put to death the hostility.

Colossians 1:21-27

21 And although you were previously alienated and hostile in attitude, engaged in evil deeds, 22 yet He has now reconciled you in His body of flesh through death, in order to present you before Him holy and blameless and beyond reproach— 23 if indeed you continue in the faith firmly established and steadfast, and not shifting from the ==hope== of the gospel that you have heard, which was proclaimed in all creation under heaven, and of which I, Paul, was made a minister. 24 Now I rejoice in my sufferings for your sake, and in my flesh I am supplementing what is lacking in Christ's afflictions in behalf of His body, which is the church. 25 I was made a minister of this church according to the commission from God granted to me for your benefit, so that I might fully carry out the preaching of the word of God, 26 that is, the mystery which had been hidden from the past ages and generations, but now has been revealed to His saints, 27 to whom God willed to make known what the wealth of the glory of this mystery among the Gentiles is, the mystery that is Christ in you, the hope of glory.

Reflection

How does God's inclusion of the nations in salvation give you hope? Who can you extend this hope to?

Daily Living in *Hope*

Ephesians 4:1-6
1 Therefore I, the prisoner of the Lord, urge you to walk in a manner worthy of the calling with which you have been called, 2 with all humility and gentleness, with patience, bearing with one another in love, 3 being diligent to keep the unity of the Spirit in the bond of peace. 4 There is one body and one Spirit, just as you also were called in one hope of your calling; 5 one Lord, one faith, one baptism, 6 one God and Father of all who is over all and through all and in all.

I Timothy 5:3-8
3 Honor widows who are actually widows; 4 but if any widow has children or grandchildren, they must first learn to show proper respect for their own family and to give back compensation to their parents; for this is acceptable in the sight of God. 5 Now she who is actually a widow and has been left alone has set her hope on God, and she continues in requests and prayers night and day. 6 But she who indulges herself in luxury is dead, even while she lives. 7 Give these instructions as well, so that they may be above reproach. 8 But if anyone does not provide for his own, and especially for those of his household, he has denied the faith and is worse than an unbeliever.

Reflection

In what ways can you actively apply Christian hope to your daily life and interactions? What would this look like?

Notes

Hope in God's Promises

Hebrews 6:9-20
9 But, beloved, we are convinced of better things regarding you, and things that accompany salvation, even though we are speaking in this way. 10 For God is not unjust so as to forget your work and the love which you have shown toward His name, by having served and by still serving the saints. 11 And we desire that each one of you demonstrate the same diligence so as to realize the full assurance of hope until the end, 12 so that you will not be sluggish, but imitators of those who through faith and endurance inherit the promises. 13 For when God made the promise to Abraham, since He could swear an oath by no one greater, He swore by Himself, 14 saying, "indeed I will greatly bless you and I will greatly multiply you." 15 And so, having patiently waited, he obtained the promise. 16 For people swear an oath by one greater than themselves, and with them an oath serving as confirmation is an end of every dispute. 17 In the same way God, desiring even more to demonstrate to the heirs of the promise the fact that His purpose is unchangeable, confirmed it with an oath, 18 so that by two unchangeable things in which it is impossible for God to lie, we who have taken refuge would have strong encouragement to hold firmly to the hope set before us. 19 This hope we have as an anchor of the soul, a hope both sure and reliable and one which enters within the veil, 20 where Jesus has entered as a forerunner for us, having become a high priest forever according to the order of Melchizedek.

Hebrews 10:19-25
19 Therefore, brothers and sisters, since we have confidence to enter the holy place by the blood of Jesus, 20 by a new and living way which He inaugurated for us through the veil, that is, through His flesh, 21 and since we have a great priest over the house of God, 22 let's approach God with a sincere heart in full assurance of faith, having our hearts sprinkled clean from an evil conscience and our bodies washed with pure water. 23 Let's hold firmly to the confession of our hope without wavering, for He who promised is faithful; 24 and let's consider how to encourage one another in love and good deeds, 25 not abandoning our own meeting together, as is the habit of some people, but encouraging one another; and all the more as you see the day drawing near.

Hebrews 11:1
Now faith is the certainty of things hoped for, a proof of things not seen.

Romans 4:13-22
13 For the promise to Abraham or to his descendants that he would be heir of the world was not through the Law, but through the righteousness of faith. 14 For if those who are of the Law are heirs, then faith is made void and the promise is nullified; 15 for the Law brings about wrath, but where there is no law, there also is no violation. 16 For this reason it is by faith, in order that it may be in accordance with grace, so that the promise will be guaranteed to all the descendants, not only to those who are of the Law, but also to those who are of the faith of Abraham, who is the father of us all, 17 (as it is written: "I have made you a father of many nations") in the presence of Him whom he believed, that is, God, who gives life to the dead and calls into being things that do not exist. 18 In hope against hope he believed, so that he might become a father of many nations according to that which had been spoken, "So shall your descendants be." 19 Without becoming weak in faith he contemplated his own body, now as good as dead since he was about a hundred years old, and the deadness of Sarah's womb; 20 yet, with respect to the promise of God, he did not waver in unbelief but grew strong in faith, giving glory to God, 21 and being fully assured that what God had promised, He was able also to perform. 22 Therefore it was also credited to him as righteousness.

Titus 1:1-3
1 Paul, a bond-servant of God and an apostle of Jesus Christ, for the faith of those chosen of God and the knowledge of the truth which is according to godliness, 2 in the hope of eternal life, which God, who cannot lie, promised long ages ago, 3 but at the proper time revealed His word in the proclamation with which I was entrusted according to the commandment of God our Savior.

Hope in God's Promises

I Peter 3:1-6
1 In the same way, you wives, be subject to your own husbands so that even if any of them are disobedient to the word, they may be won over without a word by the behavior of their wives, 2 as they observe your pure and respectful behavior. 3 Your adornment must not be merely the external—braiding the hair, wearing gold jewelry, or putting on apparel; 4 but it should be the hidden person of the heart, with the imperishable quality of a gentle and quiet spirit, which is precious in the sight of God. 5 For in this way the holy women of former times, who hoped in God, also used to adorn themselves, being subject to their own husbands, 6 just as Sarah obeyed Abraham, calling him lord; and you have proved to be her children if you do what is right without being frightened by any fear.

Ephesians 1:11-14
11 In Him we also have obtained an inheritance, having been predestined according to the purpose of Him who works all things in accordance with the plan of His will, 12 to the end that we who were the first to hope in the Christ would be to the praise of His glory.
13 In Him, you also, after listening to the message of truth, the gospel of your salvation—having also believed, you were sealed in Him with the Holy Spirit of the promise,
14 who is a first installment of our inheritance, in regard to the redemption of God's own possession, to the praise of His glory.

Ephesians 1:15-21
15 For this reason I too, having heard of the faith in the Lord Jesus which exists among you and your love for all the saints, 16 do not cease giving thanks for you, while making mention of you in my prayers; 17 that the God of our Lord Jesus Christ, the Father of glory, may give you a spirit of wisdom and of revelation in the knowledge of Him. 18 I pray that the eyes of your heart may be enlightened, so that you will know what is the hope of His calling, what are the riches of the glory of His inheritance in the saints, 19 and what is the boundless greatness of His power toward us who believe. These are in accordance with the working of the strength of His might 20 which He brought about in Christ, when He raised Him from the dead and seated Him at His right hand in the heavenly places, 21 far above all rule and authority and power and dominion, and every name that is named, not only in this age but also in the one to come.

Reflection

When has God's faithfulness given you hope in the midst of difficulty? What promises of God do you cling to?

Reflect on a time God was faithful even when you were unfaithful. How can this give you hope today?

Hope and Love

I Corinthians 13:1-13

1 If I speak with the tongues of mankind and of angels, but do not have love, I have become a noisy gong or a clanging cymbal. 2 If I have the gift of prophecy and know all mysteries and all knowledge, and if I have all faith so as to remove mountains, but do not have love, I am nothing. 3 And if I give away all my possessions to charity, and if I surrender my body so that I may glory, but do not have love, it does me no good. 4 Love is patient, love is kind, it is not jealous; love does not brag, it is not arrogant. 5 It does not act disgracefully, it does not seek its own benefit; it is not provoked, does not keep an account of a wrong suffered, 6 it does not rejoice in unrighteousness, but rejoices with the truth; 7 it keeps every confidence, it believes all things, hopes all things, endures all things.
8 Love never fails; but if there are gifts of prophecy, they will be done away with; if there are tongues, they will cease; if there is knowledge, it will be done away with. 9 For we know in part and prophesy in part; 10 but when the perfect comes, the partial will be done away with. 11 When I was a child, I used to speak like a child, think like a child, reason like a child; when I became a man, I did away with childish things. 12 For now we see in a mirror dimly, but then face to face; now I know in part, but then I will know fully, just as I also have been fully known. 13 But now faith, hope, and love remain, these three; but the greatest of these is love.

Reflection

How can love strengthen your hope in action? Pray for greater love for others.

Why is it significant that hope is listed together with love and faith in verse 13?

Hope for Maturity

II Corinthians 5:6-12
6 Therefore, being always of good courage, and knowing that while we are at home in the body we are absent from the Lord— 7 for we walk by faith, not by sight— 8 but we are of good courage and prefer rather to be absent from the body and to be at home with the Lord. 9 Therefore we also have as our ambition, whether at home or absent, to be pleasing to Him. 10 For we must all appear before the judgment seat of Christ, so that each one may receive compensation for his deeds done through the body, in accordance with what he has done, whether good or bad. 11 Therefore, knowing the fear of the Lord, we persuade people, but we are well known to God; and I hope that we are also well known in your consciences. 12 We are not commending ourselves to you again, but are giving you an opportunity to be proud of us, so that you will have an answer for those who take pride in appearance and not in heart.

II Corinthians 10:13-18
13 But we will not boast beyond our measure, but within the measure of the domain which God assigned to us as a measure, to reach even as far as you. 14 For we are not overextending ourselves, as if we did not reach to you, for we were the first to come even as far as you in the gospel of Christ; 15 not boasting beyond our measure, that is, in other people's labors, but with the hope that as your faith grows, we will be, within our domain, enlarged even more by you, 16 so as to preach the gospel even to the regions beyond you, and not to boast in what has been accomplished in the domain of another. 17 But the one who boasts is to boast in the Lord. 18 For it is not the one who commends himself that is approved, but the one whom the Lord commends.

Reflection

What should your hope be in regards to your own maturity and the maturity of other Christians?

Notes

The Encouragement of *Hope*

Romans 12:9-13
9 Love must be free of hypocrisy. Detest what is evil; cling to what is good. 10 Be devoted to one another in brotherly love; give preference to one another in honor, 11 not lagging behind in diligence, fervent in spirit, serving the Lord; 12 rejoicing in hope, persevering in tribulation, devoted to prayer, 13 contributing to the needs of the saints, practicing hospitality.

Romans 15:1-4
1 Now we who are strong ought to bear the weaknesses of those without strength, and not just please ourselves. 2 Each of us is to please his neighbor for his good, to his edification. 3 For even Christ did not please Himself, but as it is written: "The taunts of those who taunt You have fallen on Me." 4 For whatever was written in earlier times was written for our instruction, so that through perseverance and the encouragement of the Scriptures we might have hope.

I Corinthians 15:12-19
12 Now if Christ is preached, that He has been raised from the dead, how do some among you say that there is no resurrection of the dead? 13 But if there is no resurrection of the dead, then not even Christ has been raised; 14 and if Christ has not been raised, then our preaching is in vain, your faith also is in vain. 15 Moreover, we are even found to be false witnesses of God, because we testified against God that He raised Christ, whom He did not raise, if in fact the dead are not raised. 16 For if the dead are not raised, then not even Christ has been raised; 17 and if Christ has not been raised, your faith is worthless; you are still in your sins. 18 Then also those who have fallen asleep in Christ have perished.
19 If we have hoped in Christ only in this life, we are of all people most to be pitied.

Reflection

How has hope in God encouraged you to persevere? Who can you encourage with the hope you have?

Notes

Misplaced *Hope*

I Timothy 6:17-19
17 Instruct those who are rich in this present world not to be conceited or to set their hope on the uncertainty of riches, but on God, who richly supplies us with all things to enjoy. 18 Instruct them to do good, to be rich in good works, to be generous and ready to share, 19 storing up for themselves the treasure of a good foundation for the future, so that they may take hold of that which is truly life.

Acts 16:16-21
16 It happened that as we were going to the place of prayer, a slave woman who had a spirit of divination met us, who was bringing great profit to her masters by fortune-telling. 17 She followed Paul and us and cried out repeatedly, saying, "These men are bond-servants of the Most High God, who are proclaiming to you a way of salvation." 18 Now she continued doing this for many days. But Paul was greatly annoyed, and he turned and said to the spirit, "I command you in the name of Jesus Christ to come out of her!" And it came out at that very moment. 19 But when her masters saw that their hope of profit was suddenly gone, they seized Paul and Silas and dragged them into the marketplace before the authorities, 20 and when they had brought them to the chief magistrates, they said, "These men, Jews as they are, are causing our city trouble, 21 and they are proclaiming customs that are not lawful for us to accept or to practice, since we are Romans."

Acts 24:24-27
24 Now some days later Felix arrived with Drusilla his wife, who was Jewish, and he sent for Paul and heard him speak about faith in Christ Jesus. 25 But as he was discussing righteousness, self-control, and the judgment to come, Felix became frightened and responded, "Go away for now, and when I have an opportunity, I will summon you." 26 At the same time he was also hoping that money would be given to him by Paul; therefore he also used to send for him quite often and talk with him. 27 But after two years had passed, Felix was succeeded by Porcius Festus; and Felix, wanting to do the Jews a favor, left Paul imprisoned.

Luke 23:6-12

6 Now when Pilate heard this, he asked whether the man was a Galilean. 7 And when he learned that He belonged to Herod's jurisdiction, he sent Him to Herod, since he also was in Jerusalem at this time. 8 Now Herod was overjoyed when he saw Jesus; for he had wanted to see Him for a long time, because he had been hearing about Him and was ==hoping== to see some sign performed by Him. 9 And he questioned Him at some length; but He offered him no answer at all. 10 Now the chief priests and the scribes stood there, vehemently charging Him. 11 And Herod, together with his soldiers, treated Him with contempt and mocked Him, dressing Him in a brightly shining robe, and sent Him back to Pilate. 12 And so Herod and Pilate became friends with one another that very day; for previously, they had been enemies toward each other.

Reflection

What are some consequences of having misplaced hope?

Consider an area where you are tempted to put hope in worldly things. Bring this to God in prayer.

Hope to Be with You

I Timothy 3:14-16
14 I am writing these things to you, hoping to come to you before long; 15 but in case I am delayed, I write so that you will know how one should act in the household of God, which is the church of the living God, the pillar and support of the truth. 16 Beyond question, great is the mystery of godliness:

He who was revealed in the flesh,
Was vindicated in the Spirit,
Seen by angels,
Proclaimed among the nations,
Believed on in the world,
Taken up in glory.

Philippians 2:19-24
19 But I hope, in the Lord Jesus, to send Timothy to you shortly, so that I also may be encouraged when I learn of your condition. 20 For I have no one else of kindred spirit who will genuinely be concerned for your welfare. 21 For they all seek after their own interests, not those of Christ Jesus. 22 But you know of his proven character, that he served with me in the furtherance of the gospel like a child serving his father. 23 Therefore I hope to send him immediately, as soon as I see how things go with me; 24 and I trust in the Lord that I myself will also be coming shortly.

Romans 15:22-25
22 For this reason I have often been prevented from coming to you; 23 but now, with no further place for me in these regions, and since I have had for many years a longing to come to you 24 whenever I go to Spain—for I hope to see you in passing, and to be helped on my way there by you, when I have first enjoyed your company for a while— 25 but now, I am going to Jerusalem, serving the saints.

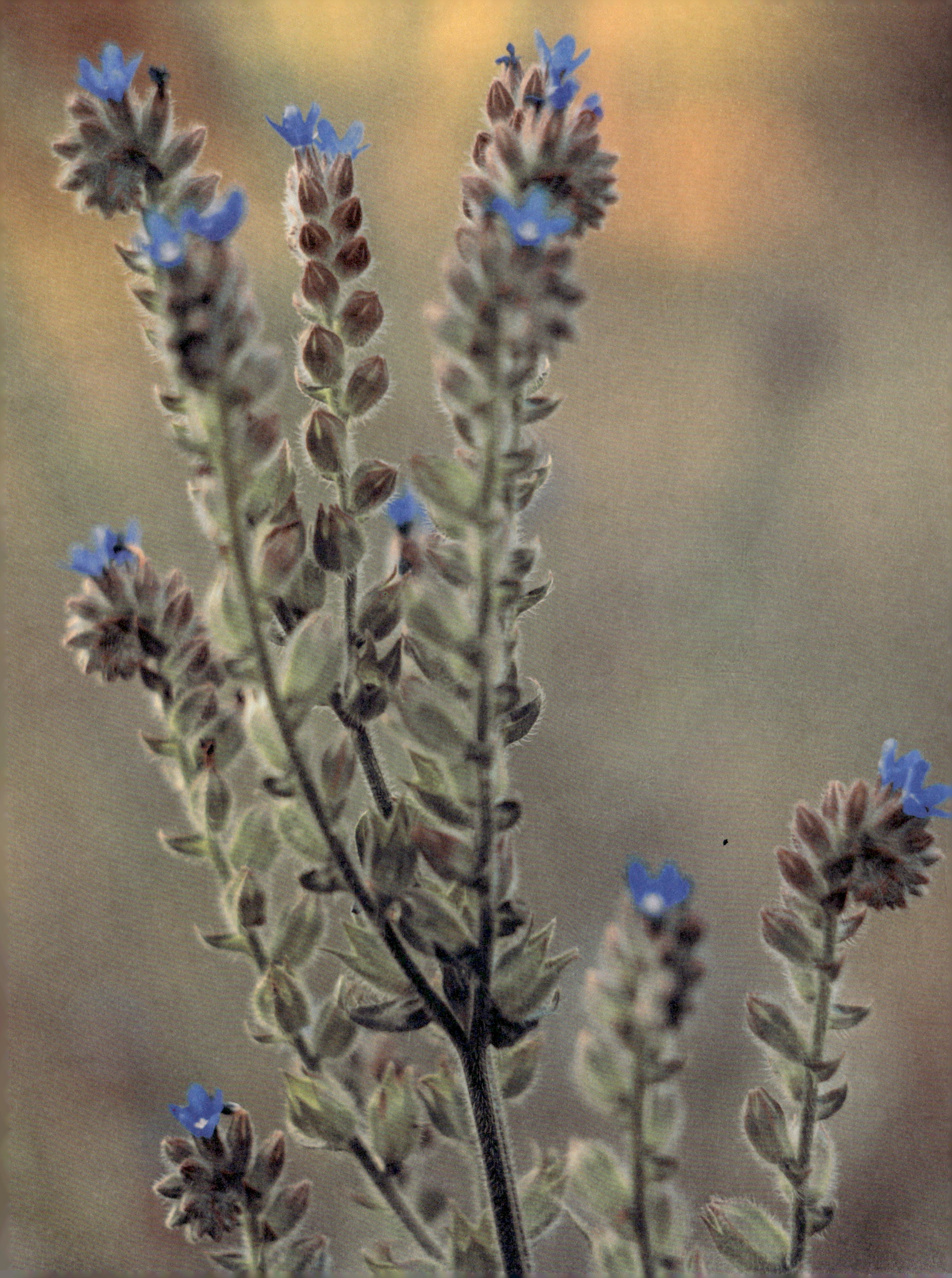

Hope to Be with You

I Corinthians 16:5-9
5 But I will come to you after I go through Macedonia; for I am going through Macedonia, 6 and perhaps I will stay with you or even spend the winter, so that you may send me on my way wherever I go. 7 For I do not want to see you now just in passing; for I hope to remain with you for some time, if the Lord permits. 8 But I will remain in Ephesus until Pentecost; 9 for a wide door for effective service has opened to me, and there are many adversaries.

Philemon 1:17-22
17 If then you regard me as a partner, accept him as you would me. 18 But if he has wronged you in any way or owes you anything, charge that to my account; 19 I, Paul, have written this with my own hand, I will repay it (not to mention to you that you owe to me even your own self as well). 20 Yes, brother, let me benefit from you in the Lord; refresh my heart in Christ. 21 Having confidence in your obedience, I write to you, since I know that you will do even more than what I say. 22 At the same time also prepare me a guest room, for I hope that through your prayers I will be given to you.

II John 1:12
Though I have many things to write to you, I do not want to do so with paper and ink; but I hope to come to you and speak face to face, so that your joy may be made complete.

III John 1:13-14
13 I had many things to write to you, but I do not want to write to you with pen and ink; 14 but I hope to see you shortly, and we will speak face to face.

Reflection

When you have been separated from those you love in Christ, how has hope sustained you?

Notes

Hope in a Glorious Future

Titus 2:11-14
11 For the grace of God has appeared, bringing salvation to all people, 12 instructing us to deny ungodliness and worldly desires and to live sensibly, righteously, and in a godly manner in the present age, 13 looking for the blessed ==hope== and the appearing of the glory of our great God and Savior, Christ Jesus, 14 who gave Himself for us to redeem us from every lawless deed, and to purify for Himself a people for His own possession, eager for good deeds.

Titus 3:3-7
3 For we too were once foolish, disobedient, deceived, enslaved to various lusts and pleasures, spending our life in malice and envy, hateful, hating one another. 4 But when the kindness of God our Savior and His love for mankind appeared, 5 He saved us, not on the basis of deeds which we did in righteousness, but in accordance with His mercy, by the washing of regeneration and renewing by the Holy Spirit, 6 whom He richly poured out upon us through Jesus Christ our Savior, 7 so that being justified by His grace we would be made heirs according to the ==hope== of eternal life.

II Thessalonians 2:13-17
13 But we should always give thanks to God for you, brothers and sisters beloved by the Lord, because God has chosen you from the beginning for salvation through sanctification by the Spirit and faith in the truth. 14 It was for this He called you through our gospel, that you may obtain the glory of our Lord Jesus Christ. 15 So then, brothers and sisters, stand firm and hold on to the traditions which you were taught, whether by word of mouth or by letter from us. 16 Now may our Lord Jesus Christ Himself and God our Father, who has loved us and given us eternal comfort and good ==hope== by grace, 17 comfort and strengthen your hearts in every good work and word.

Romans 5:1-8

1 Therefore, having been justified by faith, we have peace with God through our Lord Jesus Christ, 2 through whom we also have obtained our introduction by faith into this grace in which we stand; and we celebrate in hope of the glory of God. 3 And not only this, but we also celebrate in our tribulations, knowing that tribulation brings about perseverance; 4 and perseverance, proven character; and proven character, hope; 5 and hope does not disappoint, because the love of God has been poured out within our hearts through the Holy Spirit who was given to us. 6 For while we were still helpless, at the right time Christ died for the ungodly. 7 For one will hardly die for a righteous person; though perhaps for the good person someone would even dare to die. 8 But God demonstrates His own love toward us, in that while we were still sinners, Christ died for us.

Romans 8:18-25

18 For I consider that the sufferings of this present time are not worthy to be compared with the glory that is to be revealed to us. 19 For the eagerly awaiting creation waits for the revealing of the sons and daughters of God. 20 For the creation was subjected to futility, not willingly, but because of Him who subjected it, in hope 21 that the creation itself also will be set free from its slavery to corruption into the freedom of the glory of the children of God. 22 For we know that the whole creation groans and suffers the pains of childbirth together until now. 23 And not only that, but also we ourselves, having the first fruits of the Spirit, even we ourselves groan within ourselves, waiting eagerly for our adoption as sons and daughters, the redemption of our body. 24 For in hope we have been saved, but hope that is seen is not hope; for who hopes for what he already sees? 25 But if we hope for what we do not see, through perseverance we wait eagerly for it.

Hope in a Glorious Future

Colossians 1:3-8
3 We give thanks to God, the Father of our Lord Jesus Christ, praying always for you, 4 since we heard of your faith in Christ Jesus and the love which you have for all the saints; 5 because of the hope reserved for you in heaven, of which you previously heard in the word of truth, the gospel 6 which has come to you, just as in all the world also it is bearing fruit and increasing, even as it has been doing in you also since the day you heard it and understood the grace of God in truth; 7 just as you learned it from Epaphras, our beloved fellow bond-servant, who is a faithful servant of Christ on our behalf, 8 and he also informed us of your love in the Spirit.

I John 3:1-3
1 See how great a love the Father has given us, that we would be called children of God; and in fact we are. For this reason the world does not know us: because it did not know Him. 2 Beloved, now we are children of God, and it has not appeared as yet what we will be. We know that when He appears, we will be like Him, because we will see Him just as He is. 3 And everyone who has this hope set on Him purifies himself, just as He is pure.

Reflection

How does your hope in Christ's return and the future new creation change how you live and prioritize now?

Take a moment to envision the glorious future promised in Christ. Thank God for this tremendous hope.

Hope for Deliverance

II Corinthians 1:3-7
3 Blessed be the God and Father of our Lord Jesus Christ, the Father of mercies and God of all comfort, 4 who comforts us in all our affliction so that we will be able to comfort those who are in any affliction with the comfort with which we ourselves are comforted by God. 5 For just as the sufferings of Christ are ours in abundance, so also our comfort is abundant through Christ. 6 But if we are afflicted, it is for your comfort and salvation; or if we are comforted, it is for your comfort, which is effective in the patient enduring of the same sufferings which we also suffer; 7 and our hope for you is firmly grounded, knowing that as you are partners in our sufferings, so also you are in our comfort.

II Corinthians 1:8-14
8 For we do not want you to be unaware, brothers and sisters, of our affliction which occurred in Asia, that we were burdened excessively, beyond our strength, so that we despaired even of life. 9 Indeed, we had the sentence of death within ourselves so that we would not trust in ourselves, but in God who raises the dead, 10 who rescued us from so great a danger of death, and will rescue us, He on whom we have set our hope. And He will yet deliver us, 11 if you also join in helping us through your prayers, so that thanks may be given by many persons in our behalf for the favor granted to us through the prayers of many. 12 For our proud confidence is this: the testimony of our conscience, that in holiness and godly sincerity, not in fleshly wisdom but in the grace of God, we have conducted ourselves in the world, and especially toward you. 13 For we write nothing else to you than what you read and understand, and I hope you will understand until the end; 14 just as you also partially did understand us, that we are your reason to be proud as you also are ours, on the day of our Lord Jesus.

I Peter 1:13-21

13 Therefore, prepare your minds for action, keep sober in spirit, set your hope completely on the grace to be brought to you at the revelation of Jesus Christ. 14 As obedient children, do not be conformed to the former lusts which were yours in your ignorance, 15 but like the Holy One who called you, be holy yourselves also in all your behavior; 16 because it is written: "You shall be holy, for I am holy." 17 If you address as Father the One who impartially judges according to each one's work, conduct yourselves in fear during the time of your stay on earth; 18 knowing that you were not redeemed with perishable things like silver or gold from your futile way of life inherited from your forefathers, 19 but with precious blood, as of a lamb unblemished and spotless, the blood of Christ. 20 For He was foreknown before the foundation of the world, but has appeared in these last times for the sake of you 21 who through Him are believers in God, who raised Him from the dead and gave Him glory, so that your faith and hope are in God.

Reflection

What hope have you found in God's deliverance through Christ? How does this shape your life?

Losing Hope

Luke 24:18-27
18 One of them, named Cleopas, answered and said to Him, "Are You possibly the only one living near Jerusalem who does not know about the things that happened here in these days?" 19 And He said to them, "What sort of things?" And they said to Him, "Those about Jesus the Nazarene, who proved to be a prophet mighty in deed and word in the sight of God and all the people, 20 and how the chief priests and our rulers handed Him over to be sentenced to death, and crucified Him. 21 But we were ==hoping== that it was He who was going to redeem Israel. Indeed, besides all this, it is now the third day since these things happened. 22 But also some women among us left us bewildered. When they were at the tomb early in the morning, 23 and did not find His body, they came, saying that they had also seen a vision of angels who said that He was alive. 24 And so some of those who were with us went to the tomb, and found it just exactly as the women also had said; but Him they did not see." 25 And then He said to them, "You foolish men and slow of heart to believe in all that the prophets have spoken! 26 Was it not necessary for the Christ to suffer these things and to come into His glory?" 27 Then beginning with Moses and with all the Prophets, He explained to them the things written about Himself in all the Scriptures.

Acts 27:18-22
18 The next day as we were being violently tossed by the storm, they began to jettison the cargo; 19 and on the third day they threw the ship's tackle overboard with their own hands. 20 Since neither sun nor stars appeared for many days, and no small storm was assailing us, from then on all ==hope== of our being saved was slowly abandoned. 21 When many had lost their appetites, Paul then stood among them and said, "Men, you should have followed my advice and not have set sail from Crete, and thereby spared yourselves this damage and loss. 22 And yet now I urge you to keep up your courage, for there will be no loss of life among you, but only of the ship.

Reflection

How does God comfort and restore us when we lose hope?

Notes

Hope of the Resurrection

Acts 2:24-28
24 But God raised Him from the dead, putting an end to the agony of death, since it was impossible for Him to be held in its power. 25 For David says of Him,

'I saw the Lord continually before me,
Because He is at my right hand, so that I will not be shaken.
26 Therefore my heart was glad and my tongue was overjoyed;
Moreover my flesh also will live in hope;
27 For You will not abandon my soul to Hades,
Nor will You allow Your Holy One to undergo decay.
28 You have made known to me the ways of life;
You will make me full of gladness with Your presence.'

Acts 23:6-8
6 But Paul, perceiving that one group were Sadducees and the other Pharisees, began crying out in the Council, "Brothers, I am a Pharisee, a son of Pharisees; I am on trial for the hope and resurrection of the dead!" 7 When he said this, a dissension occurred between the Pharisees and Sadducees, and the assembly was divided. 8 For the Sadducees say that there is no resurrection, nor an angel, nor a spirit, but the Pharisees acknowledge them all.

Acts 24:13-16
13 Nor can they prove to you the things of which they now accuse me. 14 But I confess this to you, that in accordance with the Way, which they call a sect, I do serve the God of our fathers, believing everything that is in accordance with the Law and is written in the Prophets; 15 having a hope in God, which these men cherish themselves, that there shall certainly be a resurrection of both the righteous and the wicked. 16 In view of this I also do my best to maintain a blameless conscience both before God and before other people, always.

Acts 26:4-8

4 "So then, all Jews know my way of life since my youth, which from the beginning was spent among my own nation and in Jerusalem, 5 since they have known about me for a long time, if they are willing to testify, that I lived as a Pharisee according to the strictest sect of our religion. 6 And now I am standing trial for the hope of the promise made by God to our fathers; 7 the promise to which our twelve tribes hope to attain, as they earnestly serve God night and day. For this hope, O king, I am being accused by Jews. 8 Why is it considered incredible among you people if God raises the dead?

Acts 28:18-20

18 And when they had examined me, they were willing to release me because there were no grounds for putting me to death. 19 But when the Jews objected, I was forced to appeal to Caesar, not that I had any accusation against my nation. 20 For this reason, therefore, I requested to see you and to speak with you, since I am wearing this chain for the sake of the hope of Israel."

I Thessalonians 4:13-18

13 But we do not want you to be uninformed, brothers and sisters, about those who are asleep, so that you will not grieve as indeed the rest of mankind do, who have no hope. 14 For if we believe that Jesus died and rose from the dead, so also God will bring with Him those who have fallen asleep through Jesus. 15 For we say this to you by the word of the Lord, that we who are alive and remain until the coming of the Lord will not precede those who have fallen asleep. 16 For the Lord Himself will descend from heaven with a shout, with the voice of the archangel and with the trumpet of God, and the dead in Christ will rise first. 17 Then we who are alive, who remain, will be caught up together with them in the clouds to meet the Lord in the air, and so we will always be with the Lord. 18 Therefore, comfort one another with these words.

Hope of the Resurrection

I Thessalonians 5:4-11
4 But you, brothers and sisters, are not in darkness, so that the day would overtake you like a thief; 5 for you are all sons of light and sons of day. We are not of night nor of darkness; 6 so then, let's not sleep as others do, but let's be alert and sober. 7 For those who sleep, sleep at night, and those who are drunk, get drunk at night. 8 But since we are of the day, let's be sober, having put on the breastplate of faith and love, and as a helmet, the hope of salvation. 9 For God has not destined us for wrath, but for obtaining salvation through our Lord Jesus Christ, 10 who died for us, so that whether we are awake or asleep, we will live together with Him. 11 Therefore, encourage one another and build one another up, just as you also are doing.

I Peter 1:3-5
3 Blessed be the God and Father of our Lord Jesus Christ, who according to His great mercy has caused us to be born again to a living hope through the resurrection of Jesus Christ from the dead, 4 to obtain an inheritance which is imperishable, undefiled, and will not fade away, reserved in heaven for you, 5 who are protected by the power of God through faith for a salvation ready to be revealed in the last time.

Reflection

How does your hope in the resurrection change how you view death and life?

Notes

Hope in Service

I Corinthians 9:9-12
9 For it is written in the Law of Moses: "You shall not muzzle the ox while it is threshing." God is not concerned about oxen, is He? 10 Or is He speaking entirely for our sake? Yes, it was written for our sake, because the plowman ought to plow in hope, and the thresher to thresh in hope of sharing in the crops. 11 If we sowed spiritual things in you, is it too much if we reap material things from you? 12 If others share the right over you, do we not more? Nevertheless, we did not use this right, but we endure all things so that we will cause no hindrance to the gospel of Christ.

Philippians 1:18-21
18 What then? Only that in every way, whether in pretense or in truth, Christ is proclaimed, and in this I rejoice. But not only that, I also will rejoice, 19 for I know that this will turn out for my deliverance through your prayers and the provision of the Spirit of Jesus Christ, 20 according to my eager expectation and hope, that I will not be put to shame in anything, but that with all boldness, Christ will even now, as always, be exalted in my body, whether by life or by death. 21 For to me, to live is Christ, and to die is gain.

I Thessalonians 1:2-3
2 We always give thanks to God for all of you, making mention of you in our prayers;
3 constantly keeping in mind your work of faith and labor of love and perseverance of hope in our Lord Jesus Christ in the presence of our God and Father.

I Thessalonians 2:17-20
17 But we, brothers and sisters, having been orphaned from you by absence for a short while—in person, not in spirit—were all the more eager with great desire to see your face.
18 For we wanted to come to you—I, Paul, more than once—and Satan hindered us.
19 For who is our hope, or joy or crown of pride, in the presence of our Lord Jesus at His coming? Or is it not indeed you?
20 For you are our glory and joy.

I Timothy 1:1-2
1 Paul, an apostle of Christ Jesus according to the commandment of God our Savior, and of Christ Jesus, who is our hope, 2 To Timothy, my true son in the faith: Grace, mercy, and peace from God the Father and Christ Jesus our Lord.

Hope in Service

I Timothy 4:7-10
7 But stay away from worthless stories that are typical of old women. Rather, discipline yourself for the purpose of godliness; 8 for bodily training is just slightly beneficial, but godliness is beneficial for all things, since it holds promise for the present life and also for the life to come. 9 It is a trustworthy statement deserving full acceptance. 10 For it is for this we labor and strive, because we have set our hope on the living God, who is the Savior of all mankind, especially of believers.

Hebrews 3:1-6
1 Therefore, holy brothers and sisters, partakers of a heavenly calling, consider the Apostle and High Priest of our confession: Jesus; 2 He was faithful to Him who appointed Him, as Moses also was in all His house. 3 For He has been counted worthy of more glory than Moses, by just so much as the builder of the house has more honor than the house. 4 For every house is built by someone, but the builder of all things is God. 5 Now Moses was faithful in all God's house as a servant, for a testimony of those things which were to be spoken later; 6 but Christ was faithful as a Son over His house—whose house we are, if we hold firmly to our confidence and the boast of our hope.

I Peter 3:13-17
13 And who is there to harm you if you prove zealous for what is good? 14 But even if you should suffer for the sake of righteousness, you are blessed. And do not fear their intimidation, and do not be in dread, 15 but sanctify Christ as Lord in your hearts, always being ready to make a defense to everyone who asks you to give an account for the hope that is in you, but with gentleness and respect; 16 and keep a good conscience so that in the thing in which you are slandered, those who disparage your good behavior in Christ will be put to shame. 17 For it is better, if God should will it so, that you suffer for doing what is right rather than for doing what is wrong.

Reflection

How does your eternal hope and joy in Christ help you to persevere in ministry and service?

How can you balance your hope for eternal things with your hope for God's earthly provision?

Hope in Review

After reading all the verses in the Bible about hope, how would you describe the biblical concept of hope?

What are you taking away from this study for your own life?

After reading this book, we hope that your heart has grown in love and appreciation for the incredible grace and mercy shown to us by God. He has given us so many reasons to abound in hope!

Like Abraham, we daily walk in the hope of His promises. We eagerly await the return of Jesus and the resurrection from the dead. We groan in hopeful expectation for our adoption and the redemption of our bodies, and for the glory that will be revealed in us and to us.

"But hope that is seen is not hope...." (Romans 8:24) Therefore we patiently wait, with endurance. We walk in humility, serving the Lord and loving others.

May you abound in hope by the power of the Holy Spirit!